Living Your Destiny

Dr. Shirley K. Clark

PURPOSE & DESTINY SERIES, VOL. 3

Dr. Shirley K. Clark
"Strategy Coach"

How to Release the Favor of
God in Your Life While Walking
Out Your Purpose

Living Your Destiny

Dr. Shirley K. Clark

Unless otherwise noted, scriptural quotations are taken from the King James Version of the Bible.

Living Your Destiny
(Formerly published under the name,
"A Season of Purpose")
Copyright © 2013 Revised Edition
Shirley Clark International Ministries
www.drshirleyclark.org

Library of Congress — Cataloged in Publication Data

Printed in the United States

Ebook: 978-1-312-83561-0
Paperback: 978-1-312-83559-7
Hardcover: 978-1-312-83560-3

Published by Jabez Books
(A Division of Clark's Consultant Group)
www.clarksconsultantgroup.com
972424-2074 (ofc)

Jabez Books

All Rights Reserved. No part of this book may be reproduced or transmitted in any form or by any means, electronically or mechanically, including photocopying recording, or by any other information storage and retrieval system, without permission in writing from the publisher.

1. Favor   2. Christian Living   3. Spiritual Growth

Dedication

This book is dedicated to all my spiritual Fathers and Mothers that birthed me and poured into my life throughout my walk with the Lord.

- The Late Bishop Mack Timberlake, Jr. & Pastor Brenda Timberlake, Former Pastors

- Pastor Lawrence Turner, Spiritual Father

- Pastor Anne Logan, Intercessory Prayer Instructor

- Pastor Mark Chironna, Former Pastor

- Bishop T. D. & Serita Jakes, Current Pastors
- The Late Pastor Rupert Dudley, Evangelistic Trainer

- The Late "Mama" Tina Blakely, Crusade Trainer

- The Late Pastor Thomas Branch, Biblical Trainer

I am who I am because of all of these leaders. I am so very grateful to all of them!

Thank You

- Thurman Clark, Jr. ,My husband

- Family & Friends who supported me throughout this past year

- Patricia Scott, Copy Editor

- Cathy Johnson, Copy Editor

Other Books By
Dr. Shirley K. Clark

Pray & Grow Richer
Discovering Your Destiny
Birthing Your Destiny
Intercessors' Insights
Spiritual Warfare Teaching Manual and Workbook
The Ministry of Intercession
Prepare For War
Personal Spiritual Warfare
Pray, Push & Prevail
Strategic Warfare
The Midnight Cry
Empowering Your City
The Power of the "IF" Prayer Manual
52 Laws of Prayer

Table of Contents

Chapter 1
There is a Season 11

Chapter 2
Discerning Times & Seasons 19

Chapter 3
A Season of Change 61

Chapter 4
Delayed Purpose 87

Chapter 5
Frustrated Purpose 115

Chapter 6
Favor 127

Chapter 7
It's time to Ask 147

Chapter 1

There is a Season

Dr. Shirley K. Clark

Knowing that God has His own time schedule can be an encouragement to those who are walking by faith while believing in God's faithfulness to bring forth His prophetic promise. But it can also be a frustration to the flesh, trying the patience of the saints.[1] Ecclesiastes 3:1 says, **"To every thing there is a season, and a time to every purpose under the heaven."** The implication in this scripture introduces us to the fact that there is a divine appointment for all things. And it is in this scripture alone that the essential keys to obtaining your destiny are found. They are "seasons," "purpose" and "timing." All of these keys are

> *In order for the favor of God to be upon your life and to be able to live out your destiny, you must be in a season of purpose.*

critical when in a season of purpose. Coming into the full understanding of the operation of these three keys can shift your life into another dimension.

God moves in seasons and times -- **"And God said, let there be lights in the firmament of the heaven to divide the day from the night; and let them be for signs, and for seasons,**

and for days, and years" (Genesis 1:14), but with the seasons and times, there must always be a corresponding purpose.

In order for the favor of God to be upon your life and to be able to live out your destiny, you must be in a season of purpose; for it is purpose that the favor of God rests upon. ***Proverbs 14:35 says it this way, "The King's favour is toward a wise servant: but his wrath is against him that causeth shame."***

It is the wise servant that understands the seasons and timings of God. It is the wise servant that understands purpose. God will release favor toward those who walk in purpose. The purpose of God can and will only be worked out in His season and timing.

Jeremiah the prophet declares it this way, ***"For I know the thoughts that I have for you...thoughts of peace not of evil, to give you an expected end."*** God knows how your ending will be defined. He is all knowing. He ordained your ending when He orchestrated your beginning. In 1 Samuel, God told Samuel in Chapter 3, Verse 12, when I begin a thing, I will also make an end.

God never starts anything He cannot finish. He is a finisher. He is the

Alpha and Omega, the first and the last, the beginning and the end.

The book of Hebrews says it this way; He is also the author and finisher of our faith. Know that God has purpose for your life, but it can only be released in the proper season and time.

Dr. Shirley K. Clark

Chapter 2

Discerning Times & Seasons

Dr. Shirley K. Clark

Discernment essentially has a lot to do with wisdom. Exercising wisdom in judging spiritual activities or spiritual matters is absolutely vital for our sustainability and integrity in regards to understanding the timing of God and walking out our destiny. Unless we can consistently and reliably determine the times and seasons of God's dealing, we, most likely, will find ourselves operating in some form or fashion that is not congruent with the current season that we are in. As a result, we run a high risk in being deceived or ending up frustrated. Every Christian needs to strengthen their discernment.

¹Blessed is the man that walketh not in the counsel of the ungodly, nor standeth in the way of sinners, nor sitteth in the seat of the scornful.

²But his delight is in the law of the Lord; and in his law doth he meditate day and night.

³And he shall be like a tree planted by the rivers of water, **that bringeth forth his fruit in his season;** *his leaf also shall not wither; and whatsoever he doeth shall prosper.*

Psalms 1:1-3

Constantly, there is spiritual activity within our lives; therefore, we need discernment to discern the source of this activity, so we can continue to walk out our destiny. There is good spiritual activity and there is bad spiritual activity. Discernment of spirits or spiritual activity is a necessity in our lives if we are going to prosper and see the fullness of God worked out in our lives.

Discerning of spirits goes beyond our natural abilities. It is a supernatural gift from God. According to Jim Goll in his book, <u>The Seer,</u> discernment of spirits is the supernatural capacity to judge whether the spirit in operation has a source that is human, demonic or divine. It is the enablement to recognize the identity of the spirits which are behind different manifestations or activities. Discerning of spirits gives insight into the spiritual realm. Moreover, it is the gift of the Spirit to perceive what is in the spirit.

<u>Discern</u> means to perceive or recognize; make out clearly; recognize the difference, a clear discrimination or judging.

Here are some things about discernment in the scriptures:

- <u>Strong meat belongs to those with discernment</u> – "But strong meat belongeth to them that are of full age, even those who by reason of use have their senses exercised to discern both good and evil." Hebrews 5:14

- <u>Solomon prayed for an understanding heart</u> – "Give therefore thy servant an understanding heart…"
I Kings 3:9

- <u>There is a gift of discernment</u> – "To another the working of miracles; to another prophecy; to another discerning of spirits…" I Corinthians 12:10

- <u>A wise man can discern time and judgment</u> – "…and a wise man's heart discerneth both time and judgment." Ecclesiastes 8:5

- <u>Spiritual things can only be discerned by the Spirit</u> – "But the natural man receiveth not the things of the Spirit of God: for they are foolishness unto him: neither can he know them, because they are spiritually discerned."
I Corinthians 2:14

- <u>The Word of God is a discerner of thoughts</u> – "For the word of God is quick, and powerful, and sharper than any twoedged sword, piercing even to the dividing asunder of soul and spirit, and of the joints and marrow, and is a discerner of the thoughts and intents of the heart."
Hebrews 4:12

Understanding Numerology

When God speaks in our lives and there are numerical connotations, know that there is a symbolic meaning that must be interpreted in order for you to fully understand what

God is trying to say at that time. "To every thing there is a season, and a time to every purpose under the heaven." Ecclesiastes 3:1

According to one of the greatest teachers ever lived in the 21st century, Dr. Fuchsia Pickett, God has been called the "The Great Geometrician." God does everything according to a plan, time, weight, measure and number. Understanding how numerology plays in the scope of prayer and living out your destiny is critical in the timing of God. First of all, let's look at some of the most common numbers we find in the scriptures.

One: Symbolizes the number for God; unity of God (Genesis 1:1)

Examples:

1. "In the beginning God...."
2. The Candlestick had seven branches, but one candlestick

Two: Stands for the number for Jesus; union & witness (John 20:17, Ephesians 5:31-32; Mark 6:7)

Examples:

1. The union of marriage – "and they shall be one flesh" (Genesis 2:23-24)

2. "...the Lord appointed other seventy...sent them two and two"   (Luke 10:1)

3. The Bible contains two verses of two words each (John 11:35 and I Thessalonians 5:16)

4. Esau and Jacob

5. Isaac and Ishmael

6. Two Testaments in the Bible (Old and New)

7. There are two births: The flesh and the Spirit (John 3:1-6)

8. Two books in the Bible names after women: Ruth and Esther

Three: Speaks of the Trinity (Mark 3:29)

Examples:

1. We have three enemies: The world, the flesh and the devil
2. Jesus is the Way, The Truth and the Life
3. Three primary colors: Red, Blue and Yellow
4. Time is divided into three segments: Past, Present and Future
5. There are three feasts: Passover, Pentecost and Tabernacle
6. Three divisions in the Tabernacle of Moses:

The Holiest of Holy, The Inner Court and the Outer Court

Four: Number for the natural man (Genesis 2:7)

Examples:

1. Four compass points: North, South, East and West
2. The New Jerusalem is foursquare
3. There are four elements: The earth, air, fire and water
4. Four Gospels in the Bible: Matthew, Mark, Luke and John

Five: Symbolizes redemption; grace (Acts 20:32)

Examples:

1. Five pillars were at the door of the Tabernacle (Exodus 26:37)
2. There were five wise and five foolish virgins
3. Jesus fed the multitude with five loaves
4. David took five smooth stones from the brook
5. There are five books of the Law in the Bible: Genesis, Exodus, Leviticus, Numbers and Deuteronomy

Six: Number for Satan; man (Matthew 10:22-25)

Examples:

1. The antichrist number is 666

2. Man was mad on the sixth day

3. The land was to be sown for six years and rest on the seventh

4. The children of Israel marched around Jericho six day before the walls fell down

Seven: Number for Divine or spiritual perfection (Hebrews 6:1-2; Judges 14)

Examples:

1. Christ made seven statements on the cross
2. The Sabbath was the seventh day
3. There were seven days of grace after Noah entered the ark
4. There were seven years of plenty and seven years of famine in Egypt
5. Seven wounds were inflicted upon Jesus
6. There are seven days in a week

7. There are seven things that God hates
8. There are seven churches in Revelation that John addressed
9. Seven seals and seven books in Revelation

Eight: Number for new order (Luke 2:21)

Examples:

1. The New Heaven and New Earth will be on the eighth dispensation
2. The eighth day is the beginning of a new week

3. Noah was the eighth person
4. David was the eighth son of Jesse

Nine: Manifestation of the Spirit; finality, fullness – God operating in our natural being (Nine gifs of the spirit – I Corinthians 12:8-10)

Examples:

1. Nine gifts of the Spirit
2. Nine fruit of the Spirit

Ten: Number for the redeemed church; worldly completion, judgment (Revelation 3:7-13)

Examples:

1. Ten lepers were healed by Jesus
2. Ten talents were given
3. Ten virgins waited for the bridegroom
4. Ten plagues God sent against Egypt

Eleven: Number for this organization, lawlessness, Antichrist (Daniel 7:24: Genesis 32:22)

Twelve: Number for government; rulership, apostolic fullness (Nehemiah 3-12, Exodus 28:21; Matthew 10:2-5)

Examples:

1. Twelve tribes of Israel
2. Twelve stones in the high priest breastplate
3. Jesus went to the temple when He was twelve years old
4. Twelve spies were sent to spy out the land
5. Twelve gates of Jerusalem found in Nehemiah
6. Twelve months in a year

Thirteen: Means rebellion, apostasy (Genesis 14:4)

Examples:

1. Ishmael was thirteen

years old when he was circumcised

2. The dragon is mentioned thirteen times in the Revelation

3. The people rebelled in the thirteenth year (Genesis 14:4)

Forty: Number for probation; testing (Matthew 4:1-11)

Examples:

1. Moses was in the desert for forty years

2. Rain fell for forty days and nights

3. Children of Israel wondered in the wilderness for forty years

4. Elijah fasted for forty days and nights

5. Jesus was tempted for forty days

6. Nineveh was given forty day to repent

Fifty: Number for Pentecost; Jubilee (Acts 2:1)

Examples:

1. In the fiftieth year all debts were considered paid

2. The number for Pentecost when Christ baptized the church in the Holy Ghost

Hundred: Speaks of maturity; full count; end of all flesh (Maturity of believers – Hebrews 5:11-14)

Examples:

1. One hundred-fold blessings are mentioned in the Bible
2. Abraham honored and served God one hundred years
3. The shepherd had one hundred sheep, one went astray

God's Timetable

Also, God's language of time carries different meanings than ours. For example:

> "Daniel answered and said, Blessed be the name of God for ever and ever for wisdom and might are his: **And he changeth the times and the seasons**: he removeth kings, and setteth up kings: he giveth knowledge to them that know understanding. He revealeth the deep and secret things: he knoweth what is in the darkness, and the light dwelleth with him.
> Daniel 2:20-22

1. There are two different words for "time" in Greek:

   Chronos (GK) – It denotes a space of time or a succession of time.

   <u>Scripture Reference:</u> "Then Herod, when he had privily called the wise men, enquired of them diligently what time the star appeared."
   Matthew 2:7

   Kairos (GK) – It means a primary due measure or proportion, when used of time, signified a fixed or definite period, a season.

<u>Scripture Reference:</u> "For when we were yet without strength, in due time Christ died for the ungodly."

Romans 5:6

Contrast between the two: Chronos implies duration of a period of time, whether short or long. Karios stresses time as marked by certain features.

According to Vine's Dictionary, Chronos marks *quantity* and kairos marks *quality*.

Chronos means delay, while Kairos means a specific season.

Only God knows how long it will take (chronos) for a prayer to be answer, but when He releases an answer, it is in the appointed season (Kairos).

As intercessors, we should be pursuing God's kairos moments. God has a definite time for the fullness of all things.

2. Different Types of Seasons

"And let us not be weary in well doing: for in due season we shall reap, if we faint not."

Galatians 6:9

Each season is characterized by specific characteristics and qualities. No matter what season we are in, we should be producing a product. This is an important element to grasp in regards to prayer and walking out your destiny. **The fullness of a prayer does not have to occur or exist for you to be fruitful.**

The development stages are what we are most challenged with in our lives.

Kairos time operates within the seasons.

3. Directions During the Dry Seasons

Occasionally, in our life, while we are waiting for our expected promise to manifest, we feel like God is silent and/or we are in a barren season. This can be a very pressure moment for us to get out of the will of God. When we feel that God is not speaking to us, we must realize even the more that we walk by faith and not by sight. It is in these times that we must let our faith guide our actions. I know this is not always easy for believers, so listed below are some of the things that need to be considered that can help us when going through a dry or barren season in our lives.

- Stick with what you already know.

    So many times we pull away from the things that have sustained us to this point when going through dry seasons. This is the wrong thing to do.

- Be consistent in your walk with God

Continue the spiritual activities in your life that line up with the Word of God (going to church, paying your tithes, volunteer to assist in a department in the church, Christian friends).

- Continue to do the things that produce a good harvest

  Don't develop bad habits (drinking, cursing, smoking, partying, sex, etc.) during these seasons. These behaviors will eventually bring a bad harvest in your life. Sow seeds of righteousness.

- Do not operate in fear

    The Bible says the just shall live by faith. We must believe God has our best in mind no matter what our present situation looks like.

- Don't over analyze the situation, keep it simple

Be childlike in these seasons. Just say, "Lord, I don't know everything you are doing right now, but I am your child and my life is completely in your hands." Don't over dramatize or over process the situation. Love on your Daddy.

- Don't compare yourself or your situation with others

God knows how and when to bless you. Your due season is your due season, not anybody else's. You are unique and what you are going through is tailored-made for your situation. It is not the same as others.

- Don't make any life altering decisions

    Never make life altering decisions when going through a temporary moment. The situation you are experiencing is transit, not permanent.

- Press in and read your Bible and pray like never

before even though it seems like nothing is happening

This is going to be hard, but doing these seasons, you must read your Bible and pray. Set up a systematic schedule if you have to, to read your Bible. It is critical that you continue to feed your spirit the Word of God and pray.

- God could be testing you

    Do you serve God only when things are going good? God could be testing you to see how committed you are to Him and not to things. What do you believe?

Discerning the Seasons of Attack

In the book, **Warfare 101,** it says: Certain events in your life have spiritual significance and meaning. Israel's exodus from Egypt had several implications. It was the birthing of a new season, liberation from slavery, land ownership and the entering of the Israelites into the Promised Land. No wonder they received so much persecution and were chased through the Red Sea! Some events attract attacks. Here are a few:

- The birth of a child destined to be a great leader for God as in the case of Jesus.

- A geographical move. Territorial spirits are assigned to cities, states and countries.

- A promotion on your job or in the spirit.

- Acquiring real estate in any form.

- When you are physically tired or exhausted. Remember the story of David and Bathsheeba.

- When a miracle has just left the hand of God for you as in the case of Daniel.

- When you increase in revelation about the enemy.

- When there is disunity in the home or church.[3]

The Bible says your gift will make room for you and bring you before great men (Proverbs 18:16). The unfolding of greatness in our lives, will bring us before or in the company of great men and women. But with this promotion will also comes persecution.

> *"And Jesus answered and said, verily I say unto you, There is no man that hath left house, or brethren, or sisters, or father, or mother, or wife, or children, or*

lands for my sake, and the gospel's.

*But he shall receive an hundredfold now in this time, houses, and brethren, and sisters, and mothers, and children, and lands **with persecutions;** and in the world to come eternal life."*

Mark 10:29-30

There will always be a level of attack in congruent with the new season in your life.

Dr. Shirley K. Clark

Chapter 3

A Season of Change

Dr. Shirley K. Clark

Walking out your purpose in life will also cause you to be in a season of constant change. However, this season will give birth to a transforming power that will cause your present situation to catapult you into destiny moments. Throughout my life I have heard people say that change is good – change is what we need. However, when change occurs, it is not always readily accepted.

It is said that most people do not have a propensity to change, but change must occur in our lives in order for newness to come forth lives. **Psalm 55:19 says, "God shall hear, and afflict them, even he that abideth of old. Because they have no**

changes, therefore they fear not God." You have to be open for change when you are in a season of change. I heard one pastor say it this way, "God is not a monument, but a movement." There will always be transition when you walk with God, and especially when you are in a season of purpose. Therefore change is not an option; it is a man-date.

But even though change is a constant component of your

> *God is not preoccupied with your past (successes or failures); rather He is more concerned about your future.*

Christian experience, God, however, does not change. Rather He has designed His creation and elements to change. There is no way around it; we were designed to have stretch marks.

So many people are stuck in their ways. Therefore, when God wants to do something new in their lives, they pull out their resume and begin reciting to God what they have done and how proud He should be of them. News flash: God is not preoccupied with your past (successes or failures); rather He is more concerned about your future.

I recall a time when God dealt with me about this. One day I was sitting at home reminiscing and basting in the thoughts and afterglow of a campmeeting I had organized many years previously. It was quite successful and thousands of people showed up for the function. It was standing room only.

But just as I was feeling all tingling and warm inside about this event, God interrupted my thoughts and said something like this, "That was great back then, but what are you doing for the Kingdom now? You can't live off of this testimony for the rest of your life."

I knew then God was challenging me or repositioning me for change. So many of us live off of or out of a "major event" that happened in our lives many years previously. Ten and twenty years later, we are rehearsing the same testimony — the same move of God. God wants to do something new and afresh in our lives daily — "...give us this day our daily bread." So, we must be open to change.

Complacency is a habitual problem that we all have to deal with one time or another. It can be a tremendous barrier when God is trying to move us from one place to another place in Him. Therefore, God has to use situations and circumstances to wean us from our present state to shift us into the newness that He has appointed for us.

Weaning is always a process of deduction. When you are weaning, you graciously take something away. This is what God has to do with some people. Because some people are so comfortable where they are, God has to slowly wean them out of their present state into the new.

New Identity for the New Season

For several people in the Bible when God wanted to release them into their greatness, their names had to be changed. Their names had to reflect the new season or the new thing God was doing in their lives. Their past identities were no longer suited for their current status or future destiny. Abram became Abraham. Jacob became Israel. Saul became Paul. Their new names were instrumental in identifying the newly released destiny of God.[2]

For every season God takes us through, there is a character change. If we do not embrace this change; then we permit our past to keep us in captivity. There is a rhythm to the movement of God and God invites us to dance with Him. When we learn to flow with the leadings and dealings of God; then and only then will we be ushered into our future destiny. There is always a new "name" for the new season.

The Church is in a State of Change

Right now, the church is also in a great transition of change. God is repositioning the church for His last day apostolic move. It is a kingdom move; which will require a shifting in our methods and our means.

When change occurs, everything has to be realigned. Barbara Wentroble, an apostolic gift to the body of Christ, says that when God brings change (reformation) to the church everything has to change. Your worship has to change. Your songs have to change. Your main services have to change. Your children's church has to change.

Reformation is not restoring the old, but establishing a new, current or fresh move of God.

Also, when the spirit of reformation comes, often the government of a church has to change as well. How the church governs things has to be redefined. Sometimes there has to be a shift in leadership.

> *God is not punishing a church when He wants to bring reformation to it. Rather, He is wanting to reposition it to receive more of His glory or to release a greater anointing out of it.*

Change means to put something in the place of something else. For the last fifteen years, God has been shifting leadership in the church, particularly, in the charismatic movement. This shift has brought about some much needed changes, so that true apostolic minded churches could be established. However, it has not come without opposition.

Issachar Anointing
While it is the will of God for apostolic churches to be raised up, the established order has vehemently fought against it. When the spirit of reformation is upon a church, there

will always be those who will say, "The old was good enough. It is sufficient and we don't need to change." But this is exactly why reformation was needed because the old was no longer effective. If it was, then God would have no need to change it.

God is not punishing a church when He wants to bring reformation to it. Rather, He is wanting to reposition it to receive more of His glory or to release a greater anointing out of it. Jesus said "greater works shall we do." The church was designed for greater works. The greater works can only be released out of a glorious church. The church of the living God was not created for the ordinary, but for the supernatural.

The understanding of this maxim or saying is what the season of change is all about. Because the church has a mandate to flow in the supernatural, then there is a requirement to know what is on the heart of the Father at all times. In essence, the church must be a church with the Issachar anointing upon it.

There is very little in scripture about the lineage of the Issachar family, but that which is recorded carries a very significant meaning to the body of Christ. In I Chronicles, Chapter 12 verse 32, it talks about the Issachar family and how they were a people who had understanding in all things. They were touted for their ability to discern the seasons and timings of God. For reformation to be fully manifested in a church, the spirit of the Issachar anointing must rest upon it.

It must be a church that understands God's ways and leadings, as well as know the timing of God. Otherwise, it will end up being a frustrated and defeated church. While God is trying to move it forward into its destiny, it will be pulled into another direction. It is only when the church is aligned with the spirit of God that the purpose of God will be worked out within it.

Likewise, it is the same with your personal destiny. When we are in the season of purpose, reformation will come to every aspect of our lives. Therefore, when we are in the season of purpose, it will require that our hearts be open to the leadings and dealings of God.

At certain times in our lives, God will require certain things out of you. Sometimes He might require you to give up certain things, other times He might require you to consecrate your life more. Sometimes He might require you to go this place or that place, and other times He might require you to separate yourself from others for a season.

The key to transitioning with God smoothly and effectively is having the Issachar anointing upon your life. **John 10:27 says, "My sheep**

hear my voice, and I know them, and they follow me." Hearing and knowing the voice of God require a people that will tabernacle with their God.

In the Old Testament, the priesthood was the only office that was allowed to stand before God and to commune with Him on a yearly basis. But now there is a new and better covenant. The New Testament declares that the church is a royal priesthood unto their God (I Peter 2:9). This not only permits access into the Father's presence, but there is an unlimited amount of time we can come and communicate with Him.

Often when change occurs according to Barbara Wentroble, it is your experiences and cognitive understanding that challenges the new thing God wants to do inside of you, but sometimes what God does have no cognitive rhyme or reason. This is what happened to Moses when God took Moses from a blessed place to a barren place to fulfill the destiny of God upon his life.

Moses was reared in the palace. He received the best

> *God can still perform a miracle in the midst of your night season.*

education and he was trained in all the masteries of the Egyptian culture. He was "living high" as the old adage says. This is how it was recorded in scripture: ***"And Moses was learned in all the wisdom of the Egyptians, and was mighty in words and in deeds" (Acts 7:22).***

Although Moses had the best in his time, it was not God's best. God took him from the palace and led him to the plain (desert). It was in the desert that purpose was solidified in his life.

When we are in a dry season of our lives, it is critical that the Issachar anointing be upon our lives. By having this anointing resting upon our lives will safe guard us from feeling discouraged and abandoned. As well, the Issachar anointing will cause us to adapt to every situation and circumstance that we lack understanding in during the season of change.

The dry season can also be classified as the night season. It is the season when everything looks black and dark. But regardless, what the season looks like, know that God can still perform a miracle in the midst of your night season.

It was in the night season that God gave Paul and Silas a miracle. It was in the night season that God released a song of deliverance for them. The Psalmist says it this way, **"Yet the Lord will command his**

lovingkindness in the daytime, and in the night his song shall be with me, and my prayer unto the God of my life" (42:8).

You have to be open for change and be willing to release the past in order for God to usher you into your future destiny.

> "And he spake also a parable unto them; No man putteth a piece of a new garment upon an old; if otherwise, then both the new maketh a rent, and the piece that was taken out of the new agreeth not with the old.

And no man putteth new wine into old bottles; else the new wine will burst the bottles, and be spilled, and the bottles shall perish.

But new wine must be put into new bottles; and both are preserved."

Luke 5:36-38

Change Precedes Miracles

When miracles were performed in the Bible, oftentimes the person receiving the miracles was required to do something different. They were required to change. Either they had to change their physical location, change their minds or do something they could not do before. For example in the book of Matthew, chapter 8, when the leper wanted to be healed, he had to change his mindset. He told Jesus if you are willing, you can make me clean. He finally recognized that Jesus was the only one that could meet His need. Sometimes we go to everybody else to try and meet our needs, but the One that is always with us is waiting for us to recognize He is ever-present to perform His Word.

Every year people make New Year's resolutions for change, but as the year progress, often these people find themselves making the same poor choices and decisions they have made in the past. Therefore, at the end of the year, there is not much change in their situation or circumstances. Unless there is a new you, there will not be a new year.

Look at these statistics:
- 55 percent of Americans keep their New Year's resolutions for one month
- 40 percent for six month
- 19 percent for two years

It is said there are three types of people we encounter on this earth: museum keepers, settlers and pioneers:

- **Museum keeper:** content with walking down memory land — dusting off the memories of the past

- **Settlers:** People content to stay in their comfort zone — never changing
- **Pioneers:** People constantly pressing into new territories — unafraid

Change is always the price for progress. Nothing progresses without change. Every breakthrough in every realm (medical, science, mathematical, space, etc.) was brought about through change. If we want the miracles of God to be manifested in our lives, then we must change by principle. Miracles rarely happen to those living in the status quo.

Chapter 4

Delayed Purpose

Dr. Shirley K. Clark

I've been walking with the Lord for over 30 years now (1979-2015), and it has truly been a journey. But as I looked at my life, I realized everything that I have ever been involved in or went through has led me to the place where I am now in God – In purpose.

There are many stages in the development of reaching our purpose in God. Here are the most common developmental stages generally most Christians go through when they get saved.

1. They receive Christ into their lives.
2. Their lifestyle changes: They start going to

church, meet new friends; they get involved in church activities.
3. They get Spirit-Filled.
4. They become a disciple: They learn about faith, healing, fruit and gifts of the Spirit, salvation, etc.
5. They begin to operate in the gifts of the Spirit.
6. They start witnessing to people and leading them to the Lord.

Generally speaking, it takes about five years to become a strong Christian. Not a mature Christian, but a strong Christian. There is a difference.

You see, a strong Christian's attributes deal more with character, lifestyle change, and commitment. However, a mature Christian embodies all of these attributes, with a higher level of spiritual insight and a tremendous amount of wisdom that can only be acquired through experience and longevity.

An athlete can be strong, but it does not mean he or she is mature or wise. For example, Mike Tyson, former heavy weight champion in the world, was known for his enormous strength and muscles, but because of a lack of maturity in his life, some reported, in some areas, he made a lot of unwise decisions. So, there is a difference.

As a Christian, you go through quite a few transitions. One of the biggest transitions you will probably encounter will usually come around your fifth year in the Lord. This is when Christians begin to get a "little antsy," and this is especially true when certain things do not come to pass when they think they should. And this cause of unrest can usually be traced back to a word of prophecy that was spoken over their lives or something has not been fulfilled.

When the prophetic word was

spoken over their lives, they realized that greatness was within them and that God wanted to use them, so they couldn't wait to operate in this word. The excitement that was elicited from hearing the prophecy often causes them to want the word to come to pass immediately, and when it does not, they become anxious and fretful.

> *Being in a season of purpose is not being in a lot of activities.*

While this is a wonderful time in most Christians' lives, it is also a challenging time for many; especially in regard to staying focused. And because they want the destiny of God to come forth in their lives, they often overextend themselves by getting involved in too many activities.

Being in a season of purpose is not being in a lot of activities. One of the misconceptions to being in a season of purpose is equating activity to spirituality. Activity does not equate to spirituality.

When you are in a season of purpose, you have to be careful that you don't add things into the equation that God did not instruct you to do so. What you have to come to terms with is that each developmental stage *is* a component in your season of purpose, and doing more will not cause the purpose of God to come forth in your life any quicker. However, this is usually a sign exhibited by most people who are struggling to know the purpose of God for their lives or (here is the big one) feel that the purpose of God is delayed.

When people go through this, they often feel they have to be with this prophet or that prophet. They have to start this program or be a part of this organization. They have to be with this person or that person. What they are doing in reality, though, is trying to use activities to compensate for the purpose of God. However, the purpose of God for your life is attached only to the prophetic word that is governing your life, not activities. If you remember to keep this in mind, you will not be so easily distracted.

Process Vs. Purpose

When we are in a process of change many people cannot discern or understand purpose over process. You see the greatest opposition is between points — the prophecy and the promise. But just because you have been waiting on God a long time to do something does not mean you cannot have a sudden experience. You have to perceive and believe that the state you are in is able to bring you into victory because of the prophetic word over your life.

The process is the pruning and brooding state. It is in this stage that life is given to the prophetic word over your life. In other word, this is stage that things are birthed out of. Remember, process is what we go through and the promise is what we are destined to obtain.

It Is A Set Time

The word "season" means division of the year; and a customary time for something to take place.[4] It is a designated time, an appointed time for something to happen. In the natural there are four seasons: Fall, Winter, Spring and Summer.

When you think of the Fall season, you think of change. This is the season that the leaves on trees begin to change color. It is a transitional season. When you consider the Winter season, cold, drab and bleak things come to mind. When you think of the Spring season planting comes to mind. It is the season for sowing. This is also the season that is the forerunner for summer intrigues. Summer, of course, is the reaping season. It is the season that fruit is borne and harvested. It is the respite and joyful season.

Your walk in Christ is paralleled to the four seasons. As there are different attributes for each season, your walk in Christ varies in characteristics as well. Each developmental stage has its own form and shape. The Fall season is your transforming and molding season. You will be forever evolving into what God wants you to be in life.

The Winter season is the season that is often referred to as your wilderness experiences. The trials and tribulations that you go through are your wilderness experiences. They are your testing and refining times. These are also your character building exercises and God will use them, if need be, to redirect your life back into purpose. Remember, in the book of Exodus, when Moses was struggling to know his identity and the destiny of God for his life, God used a wilderness experience to redefine his purpose.

Here is the account as it was recorded in the book of Acts, Chapter 7:29-35.

> "Then fled Moses at this saying, and was a stranger in the land of Madian, where he begat two sons.
>
> And when forty years were expired, there appeared to him in the wilderness of Mount Sina an angel of the Lord in a flame of fire in a bush.
>
> When Moses saw it, he wondered at the sight: and as he drew near to behold it, the voice of the Lord came unto him,

Saying, I am the God of thy fathers, the God of Abraham, and the God of Isaac, and the God of Jacob. Then Moses trembled, and durst not behold...

I have seen, I have seen the affliction of my people which is in Egypt, and I have heard their groaning, and am come down to deliver them. And now come, I will send thee into Egypt.

This Moses whom they refused, saying, who made

thee a ruler and a judge? The same did God send to be a ruler and a deliverer by the hand of the angel which appeared to him in the bush."

The Spring season in your life is a component of your maturity stage. This is when you begin to take the focus off of yourself and begin to activate the Word of God in your life by sowing into others' lives. This is the season that you become more conscious of the Will of God instead of your personal will.

Lastly, the summer season is your harvest time. This is the time when the joys of life are overtaking you. It is the season of reaping from that which you have sown. It is a time of refreshing. But out of all the seasons, it is the fall season that will forever be a part of your Christian walk. This season will continue to be used to transition you from glory to glory, from immaturity to maturity and from carnality to spirituality.

> *Divine purpose requires a divine season to operate in.*

However, though, in every season of your life, you *should* be producing a product. Every season is always a preparation for the next season. Therefore, the challenge is to be fruitful in every season.

God is ever working *His* purpose out in your life, but the problem is when you can't see His craftiness working in your life that you begin to take on activities to compensate for your impaired vision.

Some even build "temples" around their activities or acts or works of God, instead of working with God. Now, don't get me wrong, we should be working for God, but we need to work out what He wants us to work on. Otherwise, we are doing the works of God, but we are not working *with* God. Don't confuse activity with accomplishment.

Divine purpose requires a divine season to operate in, but even in the season there has to be an appointed time. Time is always given to the completion of purpose.[5] For example, if your season is in the fall of your life and the time for your purpose to come forth is at ten o'clock, then you can't expect the purpose of God to come forth at eight o'clock. If God's timing is ten o'clock that is the time God has ordained for your blessing to be released. He cannot and will not be manipulated.

The Laws of the seasons

The Winter — Be prepared, Hang on, Slumps are impartial — Proverbs 6:16-18, 30:25

The Spring — The window of opportunity, "Work while it is day" — John 9:4

The Summer — Nourish & Protect, Competition will come, Learn from it — I Peter 5:8

The Fall — Harvest, "In due season", ALWAYS! — Galatians 6:9-10

The word, "season" is used in all fashions and manner in life. Here are a few examples:

- Hunting season
- Football season
- School season
- Holiday season
- Hurricane season
- Fishing season
- Basketball season
- Swimming season
- Deer season

- Rainy season
- Baseball season
- Hockey season

Here are some other familiar phrases:
- A season for harvesting
- A season for sowing
- A season of joy
- A season of pain

What is all of this saying? It is saying that there is a designated time or a set moment that something is scheduled to happen. As well, there is a set time for your purpose to be manifested. God has a designated time for your purpose to be realized.

It is critical now that everything you do be done in the season of purpose. Many Christians are involved in numerous activities that are not part of the purpose of God for their lives, but they expect the "season" to come because of their works. Again, being active does not mean you are fruitful. It is only when you are in the season of purpose that the favor of God will come upon your life.

In 2004, God challenged me in this area. You know, when you are somewhat gifted, you can "make" some things happen. As God began to challenge me to streamline all of my activities and speaking engagements, there was a tremendous amount of pressure and stress that was released off of my life. I found myself resting more in God and relying on His purpose to work things out in my life, and the strangest thing happened, God began to put my name on the hearts of people and they began to call me to do this or that.

Also, when I recognized that I was in a season of purpose, problems and situations that arose in my life, overnight, God would turn those situations around. I recall one time when I was dealing with a problem with my banking system. There was a discrepancy in our primary account in the amount of $500 (in the bank's favor, of course). After researching the matter, I realized the bank did not do what it said it was going to do. Finally, after talking with our bank over a period of weeks and they would not accept the blame, I took it to God in prayer.

I told God the situation and that we needed our money. I reminded Him that any money we get, is kingdom money and that the devil is trying to take $500 from the kingdom. The next day, I received a donation in the mail for $500. I got tired of messing with the devil and I needed God to just back me up. No matter what the outcome was, I knew we needed our money. So I

> *You cannot change the seasons, but you can change yourself.*

gave it to God. Sometimes you need to know when to *stop* wrestling with flesh and blood!!! Remember, God has your back no matter what.

When you are in a season of purpose, often people are drawn to you. They will try and attach themselves to you. They will also try and attach themselves to your ministry. This is normal and the reason this is happening is because of the favor of God resting upon your life. This is part of the package. But don't get distracted because of people. Stay with purpose. Even though it looks like the vision is delayed, know that it will come to pass.

According to author, Eddy Ketchersid, in order to have seasons of success, we must understand six things:

1. Success is not an accident or blind luck, but it is a faith set, coupled with passion. **"May He give you the desire of your heart and make all your plans succeed." Psalm 20:4**

2. When the student is ready, the teacher will appear! **"...Mary...sat at the Lord's feet listening to what he said." Luke 10:39**

3. We don't have to work on the company; we have to work on you (personal development.) **"...Skill will bring success." Ecclesiastes 10:10**

4. Success is something you attract by the person you become. **"...The unfading beauty of a gentle and quiet spirit..." I Peter 3:4**

5. Your success is more related to your philosophy than to the economy. **"Commit to the Lord whatever you do, and all your plans will succeed." Proverbs 16:3**

6. You cannot change the seasons, but you can change yourself. **"As long as the earth endures, seedtime and harvest, cold and heat, summer and winter, day and night will never cease." Genesis 8:22**

Dr. Shirley K. Clark

Chapter 5

Frustrated Purpose

Dr. Shirley K. Clark

If you continue down the path of functioning out of a "delayed purpose syndrome," eventually you are going to end up in a frustrated state. In reality, you got out of the will of God and because you did, this opened the door for the enemy to come in and frustrate your purpose even the more. When frustration sets in, you will meander along in a frustrated mindset. Even though you love the Lord, there is still frustration because of unfulfilled dreams and visions in your life.

When you are in a frustrated state, you are also easily discouraged. Therefore, you are in a weaken state and your mind will dictate or override what the purpose of God is for your life.

What happens in this state is that you begin to focus on your present state instead of the prophetic destiny that is hovering over your life. Also, when you are in this state, the enemy will bombard your life with people to discourage you. He knows God has a designated

> *Until you realign yourself with the purpose of God for your life and stop operating out of a "delayed purpose syndrome," you will continue to be frustrated.*

purpose for your life and if he can keep you distracted or discouraged, he will.

If you are feeling discouraged right now, in your walk with the Lord, you are probably operating out of a frustrated spirit. Until you realign yourself with the purpose of God for your life and stop operating out of a "delayed purpose syndrome," you will continue to be frustrated.

Hannah, in I Samuel, Chapter One, was operating out of this spirit for many years all because she did not have a child like her husband's other wife, Peninnah. Therefore, she allowed herself to become frustrated over the ordeal. For years, she cried and fretted about her present situation, but it was only when Hannah recognized the purpose of God for her life that the purpose of God was manifested in her life.

I believe for many years, God had to question Hannah's motive for wanting a child. Did she want a child just because Peninnah had children? If I give her a child, would she worship it more than me? Or did she want a child just to look good in her husband's eyes? If God knows He cannot trust you with a blessing, then He is not going to give it to you. You might work out other means to get it, but He is not going to release it until He is assured that you are ready.

When Hannah recognized that the child that God wanted to release through her was not for her – **"...but wilt give unto thine handmaid a man child, then I will give him unto the Lord all the days of his life..."** – that was when the purpose of God was manifested in her life.

It was also at this point that God began to elevate Hannah in the things of God. Her worship was restored in its totality and she and her husband began to walk in unity again. **"And they rose up in the morning early, and worshipped before the Lord, and returned, and came to their house to Ramah: and Elkanah knew Hannah his wife; and the Lord remembered her" (I Samuel 1:19).**

"The house of Ramah" is a high or elevated place. It is a haven where dreams and visions are birthed out. As God elevated Hannah in the Spirit, the destiny of God was conceived in her womb, and the purpose of God was manifested in her life. I say it this way in my book titled, *"Pray, Push, & Prevail."*

> *"While Hannah was believing God for only a son, God was calling her to birth something greater than a son. He was calling her to birth a new order in the kingdom of God. The next generation of the priesthood was ordained to be birthed from her*

womb. What Hannah thought she was waiting and travailing for turned out to be a greater blessing in the end. Many think Hannah's story is only about God giving her a son, but the real motif of this story is that Hannah had to find the purpose of God for her life."

Frustration Versus Prostration

Everything you do must be birthed out of purpose. The prophetic word over your life should be your gauge. When Hannah moved from

> *When you repent of doing things according to your own mindset and/or out of frustration, then God will begin to restore things in your life.*

frustration to prostration, that is when the will of God came forth in her life. When Hannah laid out before the Lord, her dream came to pass —

"And she...prayed unto the Lord, and wept sore. And she vowed a vow...out of the abundance of my complaint and grief have I spoken hitherto." (I Samuel 1:10-16).

If you are in frustration today, God wants to move you from

frustration to prostration. But in order for you to move from frustration to prostration, you must repent and realign your life with the will of God. I am not saying you are not saved or you are backslidden, but we can all get sidetracked at times. It is how long we have been sidetracked that will determine the measure of action we need to take to get back into alignment.

When you repent of doing things according to your own mindset and/or out of frustration, then God will begin to restore things in your life. Restoration is part of the season of purpose. God will bring order to disorder, true peace to where there is superficial peace, the fullness of joy where there is little joy. Lastly, rest will come within your soul; which will alleviate the internal wrestling you had about the purpose of God. Then things will be more solidified in your life.

Here are the progression stages in a glance:

1. Repent
2. Restoration and
3. Rest

Chapter 6

Favor

Dr. Shirley K. Clark

When you transition from a frustrated purpose state and back into your season of purpose mode, then the favor of God will engulf your life again. Favor is synonymous with the purpose of God. This is one of the benefits of being in the purpose of God. This makes it all worth it. It is a release of favor for every aspect of your life. Also, it is one of the greatest blessings and privileged incentives that God has obligated Himself to do for His people — to favor them.

Everything about you will be governed by favor -- wherever you go and whatever you do. This is why it is so important that you abandon negative attitudes because God wants to favor you. Proverbs 29:26 states it this way, **"Many seek the ruler's favour; but every man's judgment cometh from the Lord."**

If you want the favor of God on your life, then you have to get out of frustration. You must get rid time-consuming activities, so you can have productivity. For many of you, the reason God is unable to release favor in your life is because your receiving channel is all clogged up with negative thoughts and misguided behaviors. You are "choking" the very life out of the Spirit of God inside of you. GOD WANTS TO FAVOR HIS PEOPLE!

Psalm 5:12 says, "For thou, Lord, wilt bless the righteous; with favour wilt thou compass him as with a shield."

Why does God want to favor you, so your past failures can no longer be a snare to your future, and that you might live out your destiny

Being in the secret place

There are some things you're not going to get until you lay prostrate before God. You have to get in the secret place with God, so that He might impregnate you with His vision

(Psalm 91). You must fervently seek God until purpose is birthed out of your seeking. Proverbs 16:15 says, "In the light of the king's countenance is life; and his favour is as a cloud of the latter rain."

It is only when you are broken before Him that you are truly made whole.

It is only when you are broken before Him that you are truly made whole. He is the only person that you can be shattered and broken before and yet, feel secure and whole at the same time.

The challenge for you is to be in God's face more than you are in other people's faces. What you are after is your due season. What you want is the purpose of God. Therefore, the mandate is to be in your blessed place. Many believers are positioned wrong. You have to be in the will of God, if the blessings of God are going to flow in your life.

- Favor will open doors for you.
- Favor will give you access.
- Favor will bring increase.
- Favor will cause people to favor you, and
- Favor will cause your enemy to bless you.

I often think about the situation that happened some years ago to Oral Roberts, one of God's greatest generals in the 21st Century. He was a mighty man of faith and vision. Oral Roberts stood strong in faith and announced to the world that he was believing God for over a million dollars for one of his ministry projects. He also declared, at this time that the purpose of God would come forth, but if it didn't he knew it was time for God to take him home.

When the news media heard about this, they began to mock and scoff at him and twist his words. They said that Oral Roberts said God was going to kill him, if he didn't get the money. In actuality, and what the media couldn't comprehend, Oral Roberts was standing on a prophetic word and because he was standing on a prophetic word for his life, he knew God was going to perform it.

He knew that this was part of his destiny and he knew this was the Will of God. Because he was in the Will of God, God favored him. God caused an ungodly millionaire to favor him and to give him the money. What the devil meant

> *Favor will cover you when you are in purpose even when the devil is trying to destroy you.*

for evil, God turned it around for Oral Roberts' good. But it was the favor of the Lord that was on Oral Roberts' life and because he was moving in purpose that released the money.

Psalm 44:3 says "For they got not the land in possession by their own sword, neither did their own arm save them: but thy right hand, and thine arm, and the light of thy countenance, because thou hadst a favour unto them." This is why you have to have a prophetic word when you are believing God for purpose to be worked out in your life.

Also, favor will cover you when you are in purpose even when the devil is trying to destroy you. In Psalm 41:11 David declared, ***"By this I know***

that thou favourest me, because mine enemy doth not triumph over me." Because Ezra was moving in purpose, his enemies that came out against him to frustrate his purpose in chapter four, in the book of Ezra, could not prosper. They did everything they could. They hired false witnesses, they wrote false decrees about him, but the work of the Lord still went forth – "*But the eye of their God was upon the elders of the Jews, which they could not cause them to cease.*" God will bless the works of your hands when you are in purpose.

Shift Your Mindset

Now, what you have to do is change your way of thinking so you can function out of the mindset that everything you do will be governed out of a season of purpose. There has to be a shift in your mindset. Literally, everything about you can change, if you just change your thinking.

Don't worry about what else is going on around you or what other people are doing, you have to stay in *your* season of purpose. Focus is so important when you are in the season of purpose. People who focus prosper; people who do not focus struggle.[6]

When people see all that God is doing in my life in public settings, they automatically assume that I am constantly on the go. This is so far from the truth. I have two young children and I am a wife also. Therefore, I can't go all the time nor do I desire to be gone from my home that often, so, eighty to eighty-five percent of my time is spent at home. The other fifteen to twenty percent of my time I have to trust God to connect me with all the people He wants me to connect or network with when I do go out, and He does.

I meet people in the grocery store. I am introduced to people in parking lots. I connect with people in the bank. I see people at the post office. Because I recognize that I am in the season of purpose, I trust that wherever I go and whatever I do; God is working purpose out of it. Therefore, when I bring all these people together at my conferences, people think automatically that I run all the time. But it has more to do with my purpose than my schedule.

> *Being in the season of purpose does not require a lot of socializing with others as it requires a lot of isolation with God.*

Other times because I am in the season of purpose, God will drop my name into people's spirits and they will call and ask me to do this or that and usually it is a privilege opportunity.

God will favor you with people. The apostles in the book of Acts found favor with the people after they preached on the day of Pentecost. It says in Acts, Chapter 2 verse 17 that the people were excited about what the apostles shared concerning the gospel and they found favor in the sight of the people. Not only will God favor you, but He will give you favor with people.

Proverbs lets us know that we can have favor with both: God and man – ***"So shalt thou find favour and good understanding in the sight of God and man" (Proverbs 3:4).***

Mary was favored by God to carry the blessed Savior in her womb (Luke 1:30). Jesus was favored by the Father throughout his life. The scriptures record it this way, ***"He grew in wisdom, stature and in the favor of the Lord" (Luke 2:52).*** God will favor you over other people. God will skip over others to bless you when you are walking in the purpose of God for your life. I like the way my pastor expresses it, "Favor ain't fair – God give you favor according to purpose, not personality." You have to believe

God for favor in every arena. If these individuals obtained favor, so can you.

Divine Appointment

Being in the season of purpose does not require a lot of socializing with others as it requires a lot of isolation with God. I would rather spend seven hours in prayer seeking God, than sitting around seven hours talking with people trying to get them to network with me. I like what Job says, *"He shall pray unto God, and he will be favourable unto him. And he shall see his face with joy: for he will render unto man his righteousness" (Job 33:26).*

It is the favor of God that causes people to be in a designated place at a designated time, so you can meet them. It is the favor of God that releases money when you need it. You have to seek God, so that you might obtain your future -- ***"For whoso findeth me findeth life, and shall obtain favour of the Lord" (Proverbs 8:35).*** It is a divine providence or a divine appointment.

I like to demonstrate favor this way. It's like being in the grocery store waiting in the checkout line. While standing in line you might be the seventh or eighth person, but when favor falls, even though, you are at the back, it will open up another line, and instantly the one who was in the seventh or eighth place is moved to first place. This is what favor will do in your life. Favor can do more for you in one moment, than you can ever strive to achieve in years.

Dr. Shirley K. Clark

Chapter 7

It's Time to Ask

Dr. Shirley K. Clark

If you were to ask most people what they should do when God is favoring them, they would probably give you a lot of spiritual jargon and clichés. Things such as: Seek God with all my heart; pray more, continue to stay humble, give more, etc.

All of these answers are wonderful and essential, but the number one thing you need to do when you are in a season of favor is to ask for what you want. Open up your mouth and ask God for what you want or need.

Matthew 7:7 says, **"Ask, and it shall be given you...."** Because I am in the season of favor right now, I am asking God, out of the season of favor that He has upon my life, to produce things for me that in my own strength I could not. For the past year (2004); I have seen God give me things that I asked for in one day. For example: One Friday morning In May 2004, I realized according to our household needs we were $1000 short of money needed to pay all of our bills. So I went to God based on the favor that was upon my life and I told Him we needed $1000. By lunch time on Saturday (the next day), God had touched the heart of a businessman and his wife to sow a $1000 seed into my life.

I needed some software for my computer and when I priced it, one of them cost around $700 and the other one cost around $350 and the third one cost around $100 and the fourth one cost around $800. I now have all of these programs and I didn't have to pay for any of them. God used various ways to bless me with about $2000 worth of software.

One of them was free from off of the internet. Two of them were given to my daughter as she attended an educational function in Corporate America. The other one, God touched a person's heart to sow it into my ministry. We have not because we ask not.

I have a publishing business and I asked God for an increase in clients based on the favor that was upon my life, and I experienced a tremendous growth in my business.

The business grew so quickly that I needed more staff to assist. So, I went to God again and asked Him for additional people to assist me in designing and publishing books, and He met this need.

You would be surprised how God answered this prayer. It turned out my babysitter was a computer technician instructor, and while attending college she did layouts for magazines and newsletters. He met this need the same week I prayed.

I needed a new computer and I asked and declared prophetically that I was getting a new computer in a certain week based on the favor that was upon my life. By the end of that week, I had a new computer.

I also asked God for a new monitor for my children's computer and soon after this, a friend of mine was given some computers from a government agency for her non-profit ministry. Because she had more than she needed, she sold the rest. I was able to purchase a monitor from her for a nominal fee.

Out of the favor that is upon my life, I asked God for speaking engagements during one week, and the following week a lady I only met once called me from Oklahoma to come and speak at her Women's Conference. And before that conference was held, I had several other speaking engagements.

I asked God for a change in my husband's employment and within a few months he started a new job. Prior to getting the job he had, he was like many of the thousands who were laid off during the telecommunications industry downsizing. However, his present job was a good job, but his hours were atrocious. He was working 130 to 150 hours almost every pay period.

When my husband started working for this company, God met another heart's desire of mines. For several months I had been really petitioning God for a laptop computer. I knew I didn't want to purchase it. Somehow in my spirit I knew I didn't have to. So I pressed upon the favor that was on my life through prayer petitioning for a laptop computer.

Well, when my husband started working at his new job, they gave him a laptop computer to assist with his responsibilities, and since he already had one at home, he gave me his. Now, I have a laptop computer.

When you are in your season of purpose, know that favor will come on your life, and this is the time to ask God for what you want or need.

By now, I hope you know I think I am God's favorite child. However, I do not have a patent or copyright on the goodness of God. The goodness of God is available to all who would walk upright before Him. Proverbs 11:27 says, **"He that diligently seeketh good procureth favour...."** **It also says in Chapter 12 verse 2, "A good man obtaineth favour of the Lord: but a man of wicked devices will he condemn."**

When you are in your season of purpose, know that favor will come on your life, and this is the time to ask God for what you want or need.

Psalm 2:8 says, "Ask of me, and I shall give thee the heathen for thine inheritance, and the uttermost parts of the earth for thy possession."

Inheritance and possession are two powerful words in this scripture. Inheritance means right to inherit, something inherited: legacy or bequest. Possession means ownership, property, wealth or possessing or being possessed.

When I read this scripture it made me think of the daughters of Zelophehad in the book of Numbers, Chapter 27 in the Bible. It is a story of how these daughters refused to be denied their father's inheritance and possession due to a technicality. It talks about how they rallied themselves together, brought their case before the leadership council, and asked that they be given what was rightly theirs. The mere fact that they asked, God dealt with the leaders and commissioned them to give them their inheritance.

> *"Why should the name of our father be done away from among his family, because he hath no son? Give unto us therefore a possession among the brethren of our father.*

And Moses brought their cause before the Lord. And Lord spake unto Moses, saying,

The daughters of Zelophehad speak right: thou shalt surely give them a possession of an inheritance among their father's brethren; and thou shalt cause the inheritance of their father to pass unto them."

Now, listen to this. This is very important. Their inheritance was available to them long before they asked for it, but because they never asked for it, they were never able to capitalize on it or benefit from it. What is available to you right now that you have never asked for?

> **Matthew 18:19 says, "Again I say unto you, that if two of you shall agree on earth as touching any thing that they shall *ask*, it shall be done for them of my Father which is in heaven.**

You have to agree with the prophetic word over your life. You have to tangibly see it in the spirit. There is a place inside of your spirit where vision is released.

**Matthew 21:22 says,
"And all things,
whatsoever ye shall *ask*
in prayer, believing, ye
shall receive."**

It is in prayer that dreams and visions are realized first. Not in board meetings. Not in conferences. Not in counseling sessions, but in prayer.

**John 14:13-14, "And
whatsoever ye
shall *ask* in my name,
that will I do, that the
Father may be glorified
in the Son. If ye shall *ask*
any thing in
my name, I will do it."**

Your ultimate goal for walking in purpose should be that your heavenly Father might be glorified. When you pray out of the nature of Christ, your prayer life will mirror the glory of God.

God wants you to ask for what you want when you are in the season of favor. Yes, I know, God will give you some things without asking, but what I want you to understand is that because it is a season of favor, He has designated this time to favor your needs.

God is not going to condemn you because you are asking Him for things that He has already ordained for you to have. I know sometimes over the pulpit, we hear that we ask

God for too much, when we really should be praising Him for what we already have.

I concur with this statement, but I am not talking about a generalization of "asking," I am talking about understanding the season that you are in as it pertains to your purpose.

It is the season that predicates your asking. The Psalmist says it this way in Chapter 102 verse 13, **"Thou shalt arise, and have mercy upon Zion: for the time to favour her, yea, the set time, is come."**

Jabez Was Not Afraid to Ask

Jabez would have never prayed the prayer he prayed if He thought God would be mad at him for asking. Jabez prayed a clear and precise prayer – that God would bless his life.

> "Oh, that You would bless me indeed, and enlarge my territory, that Your hand would be with me, and that You would keep me from evil."
> 1 Chronicles 4:9-10

The first thing Jabez asked for in his prayer was that God would bless him and make him great. If this prayer was viewed through the eye of the flesh or carnality, one would think Jabez was praying a selfish prayer. However, this would be so far from the truth.

According to Jabez's mother, she birthed him in sorrow, and it was because of this, she named him Jabez. But, I believe, when Jabez grew older, he recognized he no longer needed to function from out of this type of mindset or past identity. I believe he came to grips with the fact that regardless of his past or present circumstance, there was a level of greatness yet to come forth out of his life. Someone once said there is really very little difference between people – but that little difference can make a great deal of difference.

Jabez might not have parted the Red Sea like Moses or caused an ax head to float on water like Elisha, but because he understood the principle of asking, his life was enriched immensely. This difference was a great difference.[7]

If you know you are in the season of favor, then take advantage of this season and ask God for what you need.

> **Psalm 30:5 says, "For his anger endureth but a moment; in his *favour* is life: weeping may endure for a**

night, but joy cometh in the morning."

Proverbs 14:9 says, "Fools make a mock at sin: but among the righteous there is *favour*."

Proverbs 19:12 says, "The king's wrath is as the roaring of a lion; but his *favour* is as dew upon the grass."

Proverbs 22:1 says, "A good name is rather to be chosen than great riches, and loving *favour* rather than silver and gold."

THIS YEAR CAN BE YOUR SEASON FOR FAVOR! WHAT ARE YOU GOING TO DO ABOUT IT?

Endnotes

1. Hamon, Bill. <u>Prophets & Personal Prophecy</u>. Published by Destiny Image, Shippenburg, PA, 2001. pg. 93

2. Wentroble, Barbara. <u>A People of Destiny.</u> Published by Wagner Publications, Colorado Springs, CO, 2000. pg. 22

3. Conner. S. M. <u>Warfare 101.</u> Published by S. M. Conner, Mansfield, TX, 2002. pg. 14

4. Merriam Webster. <u>Webster's Vest Pocket Dictionary.</u> Publisher unknown. pg. 287

5. Munroe, Myles. <u>In Pursuit of Purpose.</u> Published by Destiny Image, Shippensburg, PA, 1992. pg. 65

6. Hornbuckle, Renee. <u>The Power of Passion</u>. Published by Agape Christian Fellowship, Arlington, TX, pg. 33

7. Wilkerson, Bruce. <u>The Prayer of Jabez.</u> Published by Multnomah, Sisters, OR, 2000. pg. 12

Living Your Destiny

Dr. Shirley K. Clark

www.ingramcontent.com/pod-product-compliance
Lightning Source LLC
Chambersburg PA
CBHW071925290426
44110CB00013B/1479